GYPSY CANTE

deep song of the caves

selected and translated
by Will Kirkland

CITY LIGHTS BOOKS
SAN FRANCISCO

Cover design: Big Fish Books
Type design: Isidro Rodriquez
Typography: Harvest Graphics

Cover photo of Fernanda de Utrera and Diego del Gastor by Bill Davidson,
    courtesy of Mica Grañja

Library of Congress Cataloging-in-Publication Data

Gypsy cante : deep song of the caves / selected and translated by Will
Kirkland.
        p.   cm.
    ISBN 0-87286-361-1
    1. Folk songs, Spanish — Spain — Texts.   2. Flamenco — Texts.
    I. Kirkland, Will, 1943–

PQ6210.G96 1999
782.42162'610468'0268 — dc21
99-048579

CITY LIGHTS BOOKS are edited by Lawrence Ferlinghetti and Nancy J. Peters
and published at the City Lights Bookstore, 261 Columbus Avenue, San
Francisco, CA 94133.

ACKNOWLEDGMENTS

There are many to thank, who over the years have helped and encouraged my interest, my understanding, and this book: Chris Carnes for his contribution of the invaluable collection by Fernandez Bañuls, Mica Grañja for photographs, Nancy J. Peters for her enthusiasm and sure-handed guidance, Cola Franzen, Alexis Levitin, and other ALTA translators who have listened so well and helped; most of all to Bignia Kuoni, whose courage set me on the road, and to Lexie Sifford, who keeps me there.

CONTENTS

Introduction   vii

Cante Lyrics   1

Sources   97

Bibliography / Discography   105

INTRODUCTION

In the caves of the heart where pain taps out its rhythms and sorrow sets its loss to song, where passion vibrates along its own taut strings, we are all equal. There, where we seem to be most alone is where we most truly are not, if the depths of that heart are truly expressed and heard. From the caves of the heart come cries so surprising, and yet so universal, that aloneness is shattered and we know ourselves to be undivided by race or ethnicity, by experience or history.

From southern Spain—in cave dwellings and at spark-lit forges, in houses on arid hillsides and in unassuming village bars—comes a dramatic form of expression, a singular art. Hands clap out the rhythm, throats open in song, feelings of anguish, jealousy, and desire go public. Friends and family gather and the *juerga* begins. There is no program, no intention, and no audience in the modern sense. Everyone knows the singer, the songs, and the feelings from which they come. *Cante jondo*, like the air, is a communal possession, kept alive and aflame over the years by unlettered geniuses. It is passed on in ecstatic dance and song to whomever will pick it up and pass it on to the next generation. Scorned by the self-contained, the proper, and the vigilant, nearly forgotten in the onslaught of modernity, still in danger from the corrosive force of gold and applause, deep song, the heart and soul of flamenco, survives, fed by the deepest needs of the heart.

Flamenco! The word conjures a heady image of swirling skirts, dark women with snapping castanets; guitar players making unimaginable runs on the strings; perhaps a singer dressed in black, with a strange, fierce, and incomprehensible song. Yet this is only the latest, and most showy, of flamenco's lives, the roots of which are lost in antiquity.

The flamenco I became interested in was of the early vocal tradition, sometimes sung with light guitar accompaniment, but often without. It most reminded me of early country blues in the U.S. Although the songs of Robert Johnson, Blind Lemon Jefferson, and Son House are never without guitar, the blues and flamenco have much in common. First, one either grows up with or acquires a taste for these songs; they are not "easy listening" entertainment. The lyrics are often direct reports of pain and suffering: "I got stones in my passway / and my road seems as dark as night; / I have pains in my heart / they have taken my appetite" (Robert Johnson). They are often about love — mostly love lost. Flamenco, however, often contemplates death in ways the blues does not: "Let the bells toll, / Let them toll with sorrow; / The mother of my heart has died, / The mother of my soul." And the blues is filled with sexual innuendo in ways that flamenco is not: "I'm 'on' h'ist your hood, mama / I'm bound to check your oil," or "Hot tamales and they are red hot / yes, she got 'em for sale." Flamenco seldom boasts about sexual appetite or conquest.

Flamenco has little in the way of direct social protest, even though its cry is often against injustice. It simply expresses the pain and does not call for redress or remedy. It reports the death of a brother like the destruction of a passing hurricane. Listening to recordings of some of the great early *cantaores*, I wanted to know the subjects and origins of the songs. This book is the result of my modest efforts to understand.

The origin of the word flamenco is hidden in the past, lit sporadically with bright speculation. For some, the word is related to the Arabic *felahmengu* (fugitive peasant) and for others to *felah men ikum* (laborers or laborers' song.). Flamenco is also the name for the flamingo bird, perhaps reminding early listeners of the erect, still stance of the *cantaores* when they sing. Yet others believe that since flamenco denotes the Flemish people and language it may have come to refer to the Gypsies who first appeared in Spain, from Flanders, during the days of the Empire. Flamenco is also the name of a knife used in street fights in poor barrios, and is a way to refer to certain people, e.g., "he, or she, is very flamenco"—showy, gaudy, extravagant.

As with the word itself, there has been much discussion and disagreement over the songs. While the music is said to have various ancient roots, what is now recognized as flamenco, or Gypsy-Andaluz song, seems to have arisen only in the late 1700s. The first modern documentation of the lyrics, singers, history, and music was done in the 1880s and published in 1888 by Antonio Machado y Alvarez, under the name Demófilo (love of people.) His seminal book, still released in various editions, recognized several types of song and he gathered the lyrics under such headings as *soleares, seguiriyas, polos,* and *cañas.* He admitted that some critics might find fault with this categorization, because the names were actually types of music and not "poems;" that is, they specified rhythm, theme, and the presence or absence of a guitar. A certain lyric often associated with a *toná,* for example, could also be sung *por soleá.* Nevertheless, he begged his readers' indulgence, since the singers from whom he had gathered the songs strongly identified particular lyrics as one type of *cante* or another.

Machado also listed the names of living and deceased *cantaores,* and the regions they were from, as many of the styles reflected their origins. One of the singers he presented was Silverio Franconetti, said by many to be the greatest of all the *cantaores*. He was the son of an Italian father and an Andalusian mother, with enough vocal talent to be guided for a short time toward Italian opera. To the despair of his mother, he came under the influence of the then greatest *cantaor*, a man known as El Fillo. Not only was Franconetti a great singer, and immensely knowledgeable about the *cante*, which was not yet being written down, but he started a school in Sevilla to train new singers and attract a wider audience.

In 1922, there was a second event crucial to the survival of flamenco. The young Federico García Lorca, with a group of café-intellectual friends and the renowned composer Manuel de Falla, convened a conference in Granada to rescue Gypsy-Andaluz song from obscurity and commercial corruption. García Lorca, already well known, gave an address at this conference that showed both deep intuitive knowledge of the song, and a well-conceived, though sometimes mistaken, grasp of the historical structure of the various styles.

According to Manuel de Falla, the *cante* had its roots in specific historical events: the adoption by the Spanish Church of the Byzantine liturgical chant, the invasion of the Saracens, and the arrival in Spain of numerous bands of Gypsies. Other scholars have pointed to the richness of Jewish and Muslim culture and song, which endured in the south of Spain until the infamous year of 1492—when not only did Columbus sail the ocean blue, but Fernando and Isabella completed the Catholic reconquest of Spain, decreeing that all non-Catholics be expelled or converted. At the Granada conference, Lorca quoted lines from Hafiz, "the national poet of Persia," and from Ibn Sa'id, an Arab-Andaluz poet of the mid-1200s.

Lorca distinguished between two strains of what people identified as flamenco. There was *cante jondo* and then there was the rest, which he dismissed as mere "flamenco." To him, *cante jondo* was the older and endangered music; it was made up principally of the powerful sung-without-guitar songs. He considered the *siguiriya* the perfect prototype, and believed that *polos, martinetes, carceleras* and *soleares* derived from it. The *caña*, he felt, was an even earlier type, and had distinct relation to its Arab and Moorish forebears, and he noted the similarity of the Arabic word for song (*gannia*) with *caña*. In the 1922 lecture, his poetic and musical intuition grips the essential, and paints it as only Lorca could: "Like the primitive Indian musical system, deep song is a stammer, a wavering emission from the voice, a marvelous buccal undulation that destroys the resonant cells of our tempered scale and eludes the cold rigid staves of modern music, turning the tightly closed flowers of the semitone blossom into a thousand petals."

Later scholars have claimed that the linkages between the various types of song differ from those made by Lorca. According to Félix Grande, a present-day essayist and student of flamenco, there was never a division between *cante jondo* and flamenco, but between *cante grande*, sung without guitar, and *cante chico*. He also points to the phenomenon noted a hundred years earlier by Demófilo, that the division wasn't so much one of metrics or style, but of emotional intensity. A great singer can take a *bulería* and sing it *por soleá;* a poor singer can take a *siguiriya*, add a guitar, increase the tempo, and ruin it.

As Grande has it, the connections are something like this:

Cante Grande:

Toná: a form that gave rise to the *martinetes, deblas, carceleras.* Typically, these have four lines of eight syllables, assonantly rhymed a-b-c-b. Always *a palo seco*—without guitar.

Polo: this song predated the *toná* and became "flamencoized" decades after the *toná* emerged.

Siguiriya: this song (also called the *seguidilla gitana*) shares the emotional intensity of the *toná,* and is usually sung without guitar, but has a different metrical and rhyme scheme. It followed the originating songs by several decades. Typically, the first and third lines have seven syllables, with the third sometimes going to eleven. The second and fourth have five.

Soleá: a song of three or four eight-syllable lines. It is not derived from the *siguiriya* (as Lorca claimed). It is often sung in different manners, as *por bulerías* or as *a tango.*

Saeta: a solemn song, always religious, and sung in great public processions, spontaneously and without accompaniment.*

Cante Chico

Félix Grande includes styles such as the *tango* (not the Argentine *tango*), *bulería, fandango,* and many others. These relatively happy songs, accompanied by guitar, are the ones most people would identify as flamenco, and enjoy as entertainment.

---

*Whatever has been true in the past, it is now very likely that every type of song may be accompanied by some sort of guitar work in recorded collections available today. —*Ed.*

Cante grande (or *cante jondo* in Lorca's understanding) was never entertainment—although it has become more so. It is "tragedy in the first person," according to one observer. The *carceleras,* for example are specifically about prison, *carcel.*

Popular Songs

There are other entire repertories of popularly sung songs, which also have histories and supporters. Sung in contemporary theatrical performances, they may be taken as flamenco by those out for an evening of fun, but they are as far from the *cante* repertoire as Rodgers and Hammerstein's songs in *Oklahoma* are from 1770s Arkansas mountain music.

In this small volume I have chosen mostly *siguiriyas* and *soleares,* rather than selections from the wider tree of song, although you will find a few *bulerías* and others. If the pure power of the lyric wasn't enought, the testimony by *cantaores* often stopped me in my tracks. As Tía Anica said: "I used to weep when singing the *cante por siguiriyas.* There are words that go right to your heart, you know? And that makes you weep. I wept singing *por siguiriyas,* that is true, and not only once, either, with that *cante por siguiriyas.* Do you understand me?"

I confess that I have felt some ambivalence about attempting to translate these *letras* into English. Translation is at best a hazardous project, subject to missed rhyme, rhythm, lost resonance, and fractured meaning. Here we do not have poems—intended to be written and more amenable, perhaps, to rewriting—but "song lyrics," which get their phrasing, meaning, emphasis, and effect from location in melody and spontaneous vocal outburst.

xiii

I could never hope to catch the incredible voice of the singers, the songs that open with a gut-wrenching *ayeo,* songs filled with sudden moans or silences, with vocal improvisation that comes not from technique but from lived experience. Even the singers themselves seldom find the dark overtaking of their souls by the *duende* — the ungraspable spirit of truth and meaning — that may overpower them, late at night when everything else has fled.

What I do hope to do is to present a small bilingual sampling of some of the most striking *cante* I have found over the years, with their themes of jail, bloody encounters, violent death, love and love betrayed, the loss of a mother, a brother, a dear friend, a lover. Though I am not a musician, have never lived with Gypsies, and make no pretense of being a lifelong student of flamenco, I hope this amazing poetic art will speak to other hearts that may respond.

Will Kirkland
San Francisco, 1999

Gypsy Cante

"When I sing as I please,
I taste blood in my mouth."

—Tía Anica la Piriñaca

~

At the opening of the *cante,* in the *ayeo,* the voice is pure expression. Its sound is like the wind through the trees. The *copla* has not yet begun; the opening of the *cante* is not made of words, it is made of sounds and these sounds tell us nothing: they tremble; they say nothing: they sing.... In the *ayeo* the voice is heard in a distinctive and fundamental way.... It is found as if in the portal to the day of creation, as if language did not yet exist.

— Luis Rosales

Even my soul feels the pain
of so many tears,
because these griefs will never get smaller,
will grow with the years.

Hasta l'alma me duele
de tanto llorar
porque mis penas nunca van a menos,
siempre van a más.

— *Siguiriya*

Like a small sad bird flitting
from bough to bough;
that's what my heart is like
on days you aren't around.

Como pajarillo triste
de rama en rama saltando
así está mi corazón
el dia en que no te hallo.

　　　　— *Soleá*

I don't much like blondes;
They don't know how to kiss.
What I like are dark-haired girls
'Cause from their mouths come kisses
To strip away all sorrows.

A blonde is worth a nickle
And double for the dark.
I'll have to go for the cheapest
Little blonde of my heart.

A mí no me gustan las rubias
Porque no saben besar.
A mí me gustan las morenas
Porque de su boca salon besos
Que quitan la penas.

Una rubia vale un duro
Y una morenita dos
Yo me voy a lo barato
Rubia de mi corazón.

— Bulerías

With a knife I killed her
A woman of the life
As she began to quiver
We recognized each other
And she was my sister

I just went to have some fun
In the house of ill repute
They introduced me to a lady
I turned marble mute
When I saw she was my sister.

Con un puñal la maté
A una mujer de la vida
Cuando estaba en su agonía
Nos dimos a conocer
Y era una hermana mía

Solo fuí a divertirme
Entré en una casa mala
Me presantaron a una dama
Como el mármol me quedé
Cuando ví que era mi hermana.

— *Bulerías*

4

Gypsies arrived in Corfu in 1346, in Serbia in 1348 . . . in Rome in 1422, in Paris in 1427 . . . . Everywhere they were regarded with disgust or hatred. They were accused of cannibalism, of having forged the nails for the crucifixion. . . . If they were caught in some areas, their left ear was cut off; if they appeared again, then the right. . . . Their heads were cut off and impaled on stakes as a warning to others.

— Félix Grande

Day and night
I spend in tears,
since they took my poor companion
and held him prisoner.

El día y la noche
los paso llorando
desde que al pobre compañero mío
preso lo llevaron.

— *Siguiriya*

Singing the pain
the pain gets forgotten

Cantando la pena
la pena se olvida

[— *Fragment*]

The Castillians on the corners
with their lamps and lanterns
are saying in loud voices
kill him, he's a Gypsy cur.

Los ⟨gerés⟩ por las esquinas
con velones y farol
en voz alta se decían
⟨mararlo⟩ que es ⟨calorró.⟩*

— *Toná*

---

*These songs were collected from various books in which each editor
made his own choice about representing the spoken language of the
songs. Some, as here, used ⟨ ⟩ for nonstandard Spanish, some simply
transcribed the words phonetically, e.g., *osté* for *usted* (p 11). Others
italicized nonstandard usage, e.g., *vestio* for *vestido* (p 29), and still
others rendered the verse in standard Spanish. I have transcribed the
verses as I found them. — *Ed.*

Listen closely to a *toná;* truly hear a *siguiriya;* let some *tientos* slide through the hairs on your arm. Perhaps you will sense something resembling the hand of Phillip V signing a paper in 1745— surely without trembling — to authorize those pursuing a Gypsy to enter a church and take him from its protection.

—Félix Grande

Lord High Mayor
and other fine lords,
the pain in this body of mine
is not deserved.

Señor Alcalde mayor
y demás señores,
estas penitas a este cuerpo mío
no le corresponden.

— *Siguiriya*

El Planeta (The Planet) was a smith, who hammered out silver
stirrups, bracelets, iron hoops and bars in the caves of Triana.
He is one of the oldest known *cantaores*, who lived sometime
between 1785 and 1860. He was the teacher of El Fillo, who
taught the great Silverio Franconetti. One of his *siguiriyas* has a
special place in the history of the *cante*. It is the oldest to which
we have a specific reference. Even today, only a few dare to sing it:

> I pray to the moon
> The moon of high heaven
> Oh, how I pray it to take up my father
> From where he's in prison.

> *A la luna le pido*
> *La del alto cielo*
> *Como le pido que saque a mi padre*
> *De onde está preso.*
>
> — *Siguiriya*

Go and tell my mother
Not to cry for me;
Only that my steps are going straight
To liberty.

Dile osté a mi mare
Que no yore más;
Sino que ande los míos pasitos
Pa mi libertá.

— Siguiriya

The singer who sings *siguiriyas* leaves in each line of the *copla* a piece of his soul; and, if not, he is deceiving the listener, perhaps even himself. If there is one style to which the singer has to give everything, has to give every bit of himself, it is the *siguiriya*. I have seen José Menese completely overcome, broken, a literal wreck after doing this song and I believe that if the singer sometimes reaches the kind of state of grace that the Gypsies call *duende*—and I don't know yet what that is — it is in these unique and unrepeatable moments.

—Ángel Alvarez Caballero

They went and killed my brother
The brother of my heart
The rest of my days here on earth
I will live in sorrow.

Mataron a mi hermano
De mi corasón,
Para los días que biba en er mundo
Tendré gran doló.

    — *Siguiriya*

Let the earth open
'Cause I don't want to live
If in this world I never hear
my brother's voice again.

Abrase la tierra
Que no quió bibí!
Si más en er mundo la bos e mi hermano
No la güerbo a oír.

       — *Siguiriya*

Let the bells toll,
Let them toll in sorrow;
The mother of my heart has died,
The mother of my soul.

Doblen las campanas,
Doblen con doló;
Se me ha muerto la mare e mi arma
De mi corasón.

　　　—Siguiriya

There in my bed
the small hollow she left,
the pins from her hair
and the comb that held it there.

Todavía está in mi cama
el hoyito que dejó,
las orquillitas de su pelo
y el peine que la peinó.

— *Toná*

Whenever I remember
how my mother kissed me
I almost lose my mind.

‹Ca› vez que m'acuerdo
d'aquellos besos de la mare mía,
yo el ‹sentío› pierdo.

           — Siguiriya

~

It is wondrous and strange how the anonymous, and never published, poet can put into just three or four lines all the highest emotional moments of human life.

There's a halo round the moon
My love has died.

Cerco tiene la luna,
mi amor ha muerto.

There is much more mystery in those two lines than in all the plays of Maeterlink; simple, genuine mystery, clean and sound, without gloomy forests or rudderless ships — the living, eternal mystery of death.

—Federico García Lorca,

Man goes through his days
like a stone through the air,
waiting to fall.

El hombre va por la vía
como la piedra en el aire,
esperando la caía.

[— *Soleá*]

After the husband of the woman he loved slit Curro Pablas's stomach and took her back, Pablas (1830–1870) lived long enough to sing this song:

I'm going to the graveyard
my God! compañera,
don't let me die alone;
I want to die beside you.

Al cementario me voy,
¡por Dios! compañera,
no me dejes morir tan solito;
quiero morí a tu vera.

— *Siguiriya*

Go and ask some wise man
Who is it loses more:
He who eats himself away
or he who cries his pain
   He who cries his pain
Will quickly find relief;
He who eats himself away
Brings torment to himself.

Corre y pregúntale a un sabio
Cuál de los dos perdió más:
Er que comió de sus carnes
O er que publicó su mal.
   Er que publica su mal
Por el pronto siente alibio,
Er que come de sus carnes
Se da tormento a sí mismo.

   — *Polo / Caña*

You say you don't love her,
don't even want to see her
but the path between her house and yours
grows no grass.

Dices que no la quieres
Ni quieres verla,
pero la vereíta de tu casa a la suya
no cría yerba.

        — *Siguiriya*

You say you sleep alone;
I swear to God you lie,
because we both sleep with just that thought
Every night.

Dices que duermes sola;
mientes como hay Dios,
porque de noche con el pensamiento
dormimos los dos.

    — *Siguiriya*

Everyone who hears me
will recognize my passion;
What the mouth doesn't speak
is broadcast by the heart.

Cualesquiera que me oyera
Conoserá my pasión;
Lo que la boca no jabla
Lo publica er corasón.

— *Polo/Caña*

According to Pericón, Ava Gardner was a great fan of flamenco: "She often stays after La Zambra closes and asks me to sing some more for her. Many times when I finish I can't help but see that she is weeping with emotion."

My love you come so late
and then you leave so quick,
I don't want, my heart,
such surgical visits.

Amore mío, vienes tarde
y te vas temprano,
yo no quiero visitas, entrañas mías,
de cirujano.

[—*Siguiriya*]

Of the *tonás*, very few remain — only thirty to forty are known to us. They were already disappearing in the late 1800s when Demófilo made his groundbreaking collection. These were two of his favorites.

In my life I've known
The disillusions of the world.
Others often have a look
But not the knowing.

Er desengaño del mundo
He conosío en mis timepos:
Muchos suelen tener bista
Pero no conosimiento.

　　— *Toná*

When I see you in the street
I get all turned around
That you pass me without speaking
And your eyes on the ground.

Cuando t'encuentro en la caye
Me causa gran sentimento
Que pasas y no me jablas,
Y agachas la bista ar suelo.

　　— *Toná*

The flowers cry, to see you
coming through the garden
because every flower wants
to look like you.

Al verte las flores lloran,
cuando entras en tu jardín,
porque las flores quisieran
todas parecerse a ti.

[— *Soleá*]

When I told her "I love you"
in the green of the rosemary
were born flowers of blue.

Cuando le dije te quiero
nacieron flores azules
en el verde del romero.

[—*Soleá*]

When we walk alone
and your dress rubs against me
a shudder runs deep in my bones.

Cuando paso por tu vera
y me roza tu vestio,
hasta los huesos me tiemblan.

[— *Soleá*]

These songs, to be born, must come from the singer after fighting his own voice and falling into an ecstasy of inwardness that will draw everyone around him into a vortex of feeling, wrapped round by that voice, a guitar, and the sound of naked palms beating, and surging down the dark line that runs from nothingness to nothingness through life.

— after Félix Grande

Of the two women I love
Which do I break from?
If I leave one for the other
I will surely go mad.
    If I leave one for the other
My reason will go;
I got me into such a love,
Cursed are those who love so!

De dos mujeres que quiero
¿De cuál me desprenderé?
Si dejo una por otra
Loquito m'he de gorbé.
    Si dejo una por otra
Mi derecho lo quebranto;
Yo me metí en er queré,
¡Malhaya quien quiere tanto!

— *Polo/Caña*

For the man whose love is deep
Even at night in his bed
Love robs him of sleep.

Al hombre que está queriendo
Jasta e noche en la cama
Er queré le quita er sueño.

      — Soleá

I asked God for vitality
and the little I have
you are taking from me.

A dio le pio salú
Y la poquita que tengo
Me la estás quitando tú.

— *Soleá*

Until my heart has broken
I have offered you peace
yet you come wanting war;
when does the battle begin?

Hasta el corazón me duele
De brindarte con la paz;
Y vienes pidiendo guerra;
¿cuando está la guerra armá?

— *Soleá*

One dark night
   In the falling rain,
By the light in your eyes
   I lit my way.

Una noche oscurita
   Yobiendo estaba;
Con la lus e tus ojos
   Yo m'alumbra.

     — *Serrana*

When I loved you most
I had to forget you,
otherwise I would have died.

Cuando yo más te quería,
me precisó el olvidarte,
porque si no me moría.

[—*Soleá*]

By the light of the little cigar
I saw your face,
I've never seen carnations
Glow so crimson.

A la luz del cigarro
te vi la cara,
no he visto clavellina
más encarnada.

[— *Siguiriya*]

I shot at the sea
it fell in the sand;
like trusting you:
nobody nowhere can.

A la mar pegué un tiro,
cayó en la arena;
confianza contigo
no hay quien la tenga.

[—*Soleá*]

If I don't come in life
I will come in death;
I will walk to every tomb
until I find you.

Si no me vengo in vía
me vengaré en muerte;
como andaré toas las sepulturas
hasta que te encuentre.

[— *Siguiriya*]

According to Alvarez Caballero, it is said that those who sing
siguiriyas sing them when they can stand it no more, when
not even sobbing will bring them comfort. One of Silverio
Franconetti's great *coplas* was born when he was traveling from
San Fernando. While passing a cemetery he remembered that
his old friend and fellow singer Enrique Ortega was buried
there. Silverio called out for the car to stop and without
accompaniment of any kind, with just that great voice of his,
he sang:

> Past the Gates of Earth
> I do not want to ride.
> I think of my friend Enrique,
> and I begin to cry.

> *Por Puerta de Tierra*
> *yo no quiero pasar.*
> *Me acuerdo de mi amigo Enrique*
> *y me echo a llorar.*
>
> — *Siguiriya*

So, somewhere around three in the morning — because all this time Chacón wasn't doing anything but talking and socializing—he says: "Well, all right then. I'm going to sing."

At that time of night, and since it was summer, there wasn't a balcony on Abades Street that didn't have the shutters open, and the people were listening as though to the angels. That was when Chacón was at his greatest. So then Argabeño says to him, "Listen here, Antonio, why don't you sing something of Silverio's?"

"Be my pleasure."

And I remember he sang one of Silverio's songs that had the tears running down everyone's face. Then Fernando el Herrero gets up and asks him, "Listen here, Antonio, I'm going to ask you a favor. Tell me—from your heart—can that man [Silverio] have sung that any better than you just did?"

Chacón's hat was up on a rack, and he stood up and took the hat from it, stood up straight, planted his feet, and said: "Gentlemen, when you talk about that man you have to take off your hat. Much, much better than me!"

And of course we were all astounded at the respect Chacón had for Silverio, and what that man must have been like in his time.

—Pepe de la Matrona

I went out to an olive grove
To cry out my griefs;
Such a crummy little grove of trees
never was or will be.

A yorá mis penas
Me fui a un olibá;
Olibarito más esgrasasiaíto
No lo hay ni lo habrá.

— *Siguiriya*

Just like the Jews,
though I be burned alive,
I won't deny what I have been.

Como los judíos,
aunque las carnes me quemen,
no reniego de lo que he sío.

[—*Soleá*]

I asked death
that when she did her tally
she'd not remember me.

A la muerte le pedí
que cuando hiciera sus cuentas
no se acordara de mí.

[—*Soleá*]

When I'm up on the hill
I like to face the wind,
to let it carry off my pain
and ease my suffering.

A mí me gusta en el monte
darle la cara a los vientos,
pa' que se lleven mi pena
y alivien mi sufrimiento.

[— *Toná*]

They took me out of one jail
and put me in another worse than bad;
I couldn't even see
the fingers on my hand.

A mí me sacaron del calabozo
y me metieron en otro más malo,
donde no podía ni verme
los deditos de la mano.

[— *Toná*]

The voice of Silverio Franconetti was rough, with that peculiar *afilá* of the cante —hoarse but sweet as honey from Alcarría — said those who had the fortune to hear him. When he broke into song with that remarkable voice of his everyone else lost their own. Perhaps he would sing one of the *siguiriyas* he made so famous:

—Alvarez Caballero

Any damn tongue
That gossips 'bout me
I'd grab right in the middle
And leave it dumb.

La malina lengua
que de mí murmura
yo la cogiera por en medio, en medio,
la dejara muda.

— *Siguiriya*

When I go to my room
And begin to think of you
I need the walls to help me stand...
Will it be... or won't it...

Cuando me meto en mi cuarto
Y en ti comienso a pensá
A las paeres m'agarro...
Si será...si no será...

— *Siguiriya*

~

A PORTRAIT OF SILVERIO FRANCONETTI

Half Italian
half flamenco
how did he sing,
that Silverio?
Thick honey of Italy
and the lemon we know
went into the profound lament
of the *siguiriyero.*
What a terrible cry he had.
The old ones
say that their hair
stood on end
and the quicksilver of mirrors split open.
He moved through the tones
without shattering them.
And he was a creator
and gardner.
A creator of arbors
around the silence.

Now his melody
sleeps with its echoes.
Definitive and pure.
With its final echoes!

—Federico García Lorca

When I hear your name
The death sweats come on me;
Sweet Jesus! compañera,
What I go through, loving you!

Cuando te oigo nombrá
M'entra er suó de la muerte;
¡Bárgame Dios, compañera,
Lo que paso por quererte!

— *Siguiriya*

The Gypsy *siguiriya* begins with a terrible cry, a cry that divides the landscape into two ideal hemispheres. Then the voice pauses to make room for a silence that is both amazing and measured, a silence in which the face of the turning lily glows, the lily that has left its voice in the heavens. Next, the undulating and never-ending melody begins as it does in Bach, though in a different sense. The infinite melody of Bach is round: the phrase could repeat itself forever in a circular manner; but the melody of the *siguiriya* disappears into the horizontal; it escapes through our fingers and we see it off in the distance like a perfect point of common hope and passion — where the soul can never arrive.

—Federico García Lorca

My griefs are so enormous
there's nothing more to know
I am dying, crazy, with no body's warmth
In the emergency ward.

Son tan grandes mis penas
que no saben más
yo muero loco sin calor de nadie
en el hospital.

— Siguiriya

When the daylight comes
my griefs begin to grow;
only the shadows of darkest night
comfort my soul.

Cuando viene el día
mis penas s'agrandan;
sólo las sombras de la noche oscura
consuelan mi alma.

— *Siguiriya*

Let the earth open
I don't want this life;
to live like I'm living
is much better to die.

Abrase la tierra,
que no ‹quió› vivir,
que pa vivir como estoy viviendo
más vale morir.

— *Siguiriya*

~

In the caves at dawn, when the singer is hoarse and the room is cold, when the wine is crusted on the glasses and the eyelids close in exhaustion; that is the time when the singer and the voice and the song may find their moment.

— (after Molina)

My hand hurts
from knocking so hard,
and the mother of my soul answered me
in the morning dark.

La mano me duele
de tanto llamar,
y m'ha respondío la mare é mi alma
a la madrugá.

— *Siguiriya*

If the dead could be raised
By valor and might
I would raise up my mother
Though it cost my life.

Si los muertos se sacaran
A fuersa e balentía,
Yo sacaría a mi mare
Aunque perdiera la bía.

El Fillo, who taught Silverio Franconetti, was a disciple of El Planeta. Learning from the master, he went on to surpass him in fame and in the transcendence of his song. El Fillo had a brother, Juan Encueros, who was, as the story is told, stabbed to death by another singer. This is El Fillo's *siguiriya:*

You killed my brother
I'll never forgive you;
wrapped in a cape you killed him;
he did nothin' to you.

Mataste a mi hermano
no t'he perdoná
tu l'as matao liao en su capa
sin jaserte ná.

— *Siguiriya*

Caballero Bonald tells of encountering Tía Anica la Piriñaca:

The full treasure of human passion in this ancient and exceptional singer blooms like a terrible flower with each of her burning lamentations.... The unfathomable root of flamenco is represented exactly in these deeply felt, humble, astonishing plaints, plucked from the deepest racial memory.... And she gives herself over to the song with intuitive mouthsful of liberation. Tía Anica concentrates, her glass forgotten in her ancient hand. She is silent for a long moment and then, with simplicity, with a certain indifferent conviction, she tells us: "When I sing as I please, I taste blood in my mouth."

I'm not sorry that you're going
I'm just sorry you're taking
the blood from my veins.

Yo no siento que te vaya;
lo que siento es que te llevas
la sangre de mis venas.

— *Soleá*

I leave the door ajar
in case sometime it might give you
temptation to try.

Dejo la puerta entorná
por si alguna vez te diera
la tentación de empujar.

[—*Soleá*]

Everyone prays to a goddess
Health and liberty.
I only pray for a good death
She wants to deny me.

Toós le píen a un Debé
Salú y libertá,
Y yo le pío una buena muerte
No me la quie da.

— *Siguiriya*

Death came to my bedside
and didn't want to take me;
my trials were not over yet
and when she left I cried.

La muerte a mi cama vino
y no me quiso llevá
no estaba cumplío mi sino
y al irse me eché a llorá.

    — *Soleá*

I am living in this world
every hope has died;
they won't even have to bury me
I'm already buried alive.

Estoy viviendo en el mundo
con la esperanza perdía;
no es meneser que me entierren
porque estoy enterrá en vía.

— *Soleá*

One night of thunder
I thought I would die,
Cause I had a black shadow
Right over me.

Una noche e trueno
Yo pensé morí
Como tenía una sombra negra
Ensima e mí.

   — *Siguiriya*

It was said of Enrique el Mellizo that he would go to the Capuchinos and sing to the crazy ones locked up in there. Other times he would go to the wall and sing out to the water . . . . Sometimes he would get drunk and in the middle of the night go to the wall and sing in a way that would make the hair of the baldest man in the world stand on end:

> I leaned over the wall
> The wind answered me:
> Why are you sighing like this
> When there's nothing to do?

> *Me asomé a la muralla*
> *y me respondió el viento:*
> *«¿A qué vienen tantos suspiros*
> *si ya no hay remedio?»*

When he got that way you could give him all the money in the world and he would still not sing to you; he wanted to go sing to the poor crazy ones, or sing to the water.

—Alvarez Caballero

There's nothing to see
because a boat that was there
has set every sail and gone.

Allí no hay naíta que ver:
porque un barquito que había
tendió la vela y se fue.

[— *Soleá*]

It was in Tomelloso, one day in winter if I remember right. The
cante had gone on for hours already and it was well toward
dawn when, majestically, the *siguiriyas* began. For a long time,
while two of the singers just listened, a third sang *siguiriyas,* with
power, with desolation, with terror, with violence, with brutal
delicacy. An old peasant tapped with his cane on the tiles every
once in a while, always keeping the rhythm. In his other hand
was a glass of wine, halfway between his lips and the nearby
table: suspended, in tension. The great old man was listening
without making a sound, his head lifted, without expression,
very probably without seeing. Suddenly, with a cry that was
incredibly horrible and incredibly real, and incredibly communi-
tarian and intimate, a cry that pierced through I no longer
remember what exact word, the glass shattered into pieces in the
hand of that fierce old man. We saw how his hand, his forearm,
his clothes were soaked in blood and wine. We were afraid. The
singer stopped. The old man asked him to go on, to go on . . . .
The only thing he did was ask him to go on!

—Félix Grande

To the mountains of Armenia
I must go
To drink with the animals
Because of you.
    I must go,
I must go,
Where no living soul
Knows nothing of me.

A los montes e Armenia
Me tengo de ir
Para bibí con los animales
Por causa de ti.
    Me tengo que ir
Me tengo que ir,
Donde persona bibiente en er mundo
Sepa más e mí.

        —*Siguiriya*

La Andonda, the first to sing
soleares, gave us this.

All who deserve it
should be stabbed to the heart
cause from doing you so good
my insides still hurt.

Mala puñalda le den
A tó que diera motivo
Que me duelen las entrañas
De jacerlo bien contigo.

— *Soleá*

From Silverio Franconetti:

I hope you get shot,
So you don't do with no one
What you done with me.

Anda y que te den un tiro;
Que no se jase con nadie
Lo que tú has jecho conmigo.

— *Soleá*

The figure of the *cantaor* lies between two great lines: the great arc of the heavens on the outside and the zigzag of the snake in his soul on the inside.

— Federico García Lorca

Deceitful world
the way you turn
so the steps to go forward
take me in reverse.

Mundito engañoso
Las güertas que da,
Que los pasitos que doy p'lante
Se me van p'tra.

— *Soleá*

The sheep were white and small
and the meadow green;
the shepherd who watches them, mother,
is dying of sorrow.

Ovejitas eran blancas
y el praíto verde;
el pastorcito, mare, que las guarda
de ducas se meuere.

　　　[— *Siguiriya*]

I don't ask anyone for favors,
I know they cost too much,
I put up with all my troubles,
so I don't make the greedy rich.

A nadie pido favores,
porque sé que cuestan caros,
me aguanto con mis dolores,
no pongo rico al avaro.

[—*Soleá*]

Your mother keeps on saying
she doesn't like me 'cause I'm deaf,
and I don't like you all that much,
little girl, from all I hear said.

Anda diciendo tu madre
que no me quiere por sordo
y yo no te quiero a ti,
chiquilla, por lo que oigo.

     [—*Soleá*]

You mother keeps on saying
For you I'm not that good;
that might be so in money
because I win in blood.

Anda diciendo tu madre
que yo contigo no igualo;
eso será en el dinero,
porque en la sangre te gano.

[— *Soleá*]

Whenever I missed you
the tears from my eyes
hammered on the anvil.

Cuando de menos te echaba,
las lágrimas de mis ojos
en el yunque machacaba.

[—*Soleá*]

Don't come to the forge
to cry in the door,
if you can't take my griefs away
don't leave any more.

A la puerta de la fragua
no me vengas a llorar,
si penas no me quitabas
no me las vengas a dar.

[— *Soleá*]

That night in January
who'd you go to see,
like a colt with the bit in his teeth?

Aquella noche de enero
¿a quién saliste a buscar
como un potrito sin freno?

      [—*Soleá*]

Come early my love
and not at such an hour,
the neighbor over there
is something of a gossip.

Amor mío, ven temprano
no me vengas a deshora,
que la vecina de enfrente
es algo murmuradora.

[— *Soleá*]

Then La Niña de los Peines got up like a crazy woman, drank in one gulp a great searing glass of *cazalla,* and sat down to sing — with no voice, no breath or coloring, but with her throat on fire and with *duende.* She had succeeded in eliminating all the scaffolding of the song to let in the searing and furious *duende,* friend of the winds that sweep down full of sand. . . . La Niña de los Peines had to shatter her voice because she knew she had an exacting audience listening to her, people who didn't require forms, but the marrow of forms — a music so pure, with a body so brief it could float in the air. She had to strip away her own skills and security, distance herself from her muse and stand unprotected so her *duende* would come and join her in hand-to-hand combat. And how she sang! Her voice no longer played sweetly over the notes; it was a gusher of blood worthy of her pain and sincerity, and it opened like a ten-fingered hand to the nailed and stormy feet of a Christ by Juan de Juní.

—Federico García Lorca

To your side
I can't return . . .
How is it for some crazy words
such love is gone!

A la vera tuya
no puedo volver . . .
¡Como por unas palabritas locas
se pierde un querer!

　　　[— *Siguiriya*]

Love slopes steeply up,
and forgetting, steeply down;
I want to make the climb
though it costs me much.

Er querer es cuesta arriba,
Y el orvidar, cuesta abajo;
Quiero subir cuesta arriba
Aunque me cueste trabajo.

— *Soleá*

I went to a field to cry
like a mad man screaming
and even the wind kept telling me
you loved someone else.

Al campo me fui a llorar
dando voces como un loco
y hasta el aire me decía
que tú querías a otro.

[— *Soleá*]

~

Flamenco is a tragedy in the first person.

—José Moneleón

Though you go to hell
I'd have to go with you
because being in your company
I would be in glory.

Al infierno que tú vayas
me tengo que ir contigo,
porque yendo en tu compaña
llevo la gloria conmigo.

[—*Soleá*]

84

By the light of a candle
I wept without shame;
the candle went out.
The tear is greater than the flame!

Al pie de una candelita
lloraba yo sin consuelo,
la candela se apagó.
¡Más pudo el llanto que el fuego!

  [*— Soleá*]

Lift your voice high, rosemary
and announce that the river has not
enough water to put out
the flame in my heart.

Alza la voz bien, romero
y pregona que en el río
no hay agüita pa' apagar
mi corazón encendío.

[—*Soleá*]

My heart was arrested
and taken to jail
and for no crime at all
sentenced to die.

A mi corazón prendieron,
a la cárcel lo llevaron
y sin delito ninguno
a muerte lo sentencieron.

[— *Soleá*]

~

... and now, with the imminent and inopportune arrival of the sun, at four or five in the morning, when the fiesta has been all but drained, the old men, the phenomena and patriarchs of Gypsy life, now almost myths and legends —el Planeta, Juan Pelao, los Cangacho— begin the *toná*, transported by ecstasy and possessed by the logic of their song, these solemn songs that blister the blood.

— Antonio Mairena

Friends, now there are no friends,
her best friend beats her;
there is no other friend than God
and a nickle in your purse.

Amigos, ya no hay amigos,
el más amigo la pega;
amigo no hay más que Dios
y un durito en la faltriquera.

[—*Soleá*]

I can do no more
than bow my head
and say that black is white.

Yo no tengo más remedio
que agachar la cabecita
decir que lo blanco is negro.

[—*Soleá*]

Every morning I go by
to ask of the rosemary
if love has a cure
because I am dying.

Todas las mañanas voy
a preguntar al romero
si el mal de amor tiene cura
porque yo me estoy muriendo.

[— *Soleá*]

At the banks of a river
I pause to think,
my grief is like the water
that will never cease.

A la orillita de un río
me pongo a considerar,
mis penas son como el agua
que no acaban de pasar.

[—*Soleá*]

Beneath a slender tree one day
I was crying my grief;
the slender tree was green
and hearing me lost every leaf.

Al pie de un arbito un día
lloraba yo mí dolor,
el arbito estaba verde
y al oirme se secó.

[— *Soleá*]

Beneath a barren tree
I stopped to think:
few friends for the man
who never gives.

Al pie de un árbol sin fruto
me puse a considerar
qué pocos amigos tiene
el que no tiene qué dar.

  [—*Soleá*]

When asked why he sang, Manolito el de María answered:
"Because I remember what I have lived."

—Félix Grande

At twelve o'clock or one,
when the wind begins to fly,
I am always drunk on moonlight
completely stupefied.

A las doce o a la una,
cuando viene el viento,
siempre me encuentra borracho de luna
sin conocimiento.

[—*Soleá*]

Though I tear off
the hands of my watch
time will not stop.

Agujas de me reloj
que yo las iba arrancando
y el tiempo no se paró.

[—*Soleá*]

SOURCES

In the original collections, not all of the *cante* were identified as to type. I have applied the metrical and rhyme rules to these, and cite them in parentheses. As noted in the preface, there are nothing like rigorous rules at work here, only the sense of the singers.

"Associated with" means that the song was in the singer's repertory. The singer may possibly have been the "writer," but just as possibly picked up the song from elsewhere and brought it to greater prominence.

p 1	At the opening of the *cante*	Text. Luis Rosales in Grande. *Memoria I,* p 22
p 1	Even my soul feels the pain	*Siguiriya.* Molina. *Cante,* p 111
p 2	Like a small sad bird	*Soleá.* Pohren. *Lives,* p 63
p 3	I don't much like blondes	*Bulerías.* Sung by Agujetas. *Agujetas en Paris,* track 2
p 4	With a knife I killed her	*Bulerías.* Sung by Agujetas. *Agujetas in Turin, track 1*
p 5	Gypsies arrived in Corfu	Text. Grande. *Memoria I,* p 75–77
p 6	Day and night	*Siguiriya.* Molina. *Cante,* p 112
p 7	Singing the pain	Fragment. Molina. *Cante,* p 47
p 8	The Castillians on the corners	*Toná.* Alvarez Caballero. *Historia,* p 12
p 9	Listen closely to a *toná*	Text. Grande. *Memoria I,* p 114
p 9	Lord High Mayor	*Siguiriya.* Molina. *Cante,* p 112
p 10	El Planeta was a smith	Text. Alvarez Caballero, *Historia,* p 39
p 10	I pray to the moon	*Siguiriya.* Associated with El Planeta. Alvarez Caballero, *Historia,* p 39
p 11	Go and tell my mother	*Siguiriya.* Associated with Silverio. Machado y Alvarez. *Colección,* p 192, #20

p 12 The singer who sings — Text. Alvarez Caballero, *Historia*, p 48

p 13 They went and killed my brother — *Siguiriya*. Associated with Silverio. Machado y Alvarez. *Colección*, p 193, #30

p 14 Let the earth open — *Siguiriya*. Associated with Silvero. Machado y Alvarez. *Colección*, p 190, # 7

p 15 Let the bells toll — *Siguiriya*. Associated with Silverio. Machado y Alvarez. *Colección*, p 191, #17

p 16 There in my bed — *Toná*. Blanco Garza. *Las Letras*, p 29

p 17 Whenever I remember — *Siguiriya*. Molina, *Cante*, p 112 (Molina says *siguiriya* despite only three lines. —*Ed*)

p 18 It is wondrous and strange — García Lorca. *Poema del cante jondo*, p 151

p 19 Man goes through his days — (*Soleá*). Blanco Garza. *Las Letras*, p 17

p 20 After the husband — Text. In Pohren. *Lives*, p 46

p 20 I'm going to the graveyard — *Siguiriya*. Associated with Curro Pablas. Pohren. *Lives*. p 46

p 21 Go and ask some wise man — *Polo/Caña*. Associated with Silverio. Machado y Alvarez. *Colección*, p 184, #5

p 22 You say you don't love her — *Siguiriya*. Molina. *Cante*, p 111

p 23 You say you sleep alone — *Siguiriya*. Associated with Manuel Molina and Manuel Torre. Molina. *Cante*, p 112

p 24 Everyone who hears me — *Polo/Caña*. Associated with Silverio. Machado y Alvarez. *Colección*, p 183, # 2

p 25 According to Pericón — Text. Pohren, *Lives*, p 126

p 25 My love you come so late — (*Siguiriya*). Fernández Bañuls. *La Poesía*. p 254, # 4

p 26 In my life I've known — *Toná*. Machado y Alvarez. *Colección*, p 163, # 7

p 26 When I see you in the street   *Toná*. Machado y Alvarez. *Colección,*
p 163, # 6

p 27 The flowers cry to see you   (*Soleá*). Fernández Bañuls. *La Poesía,*
p 254, # 1

p 28 When I told her "I love you"   (Soleá). Fernández Bañuls. *La Poesía,*
p 90, # 5

p 29 When we walk alone   (*Soleá*). Fernández Bañuls. *La Poesía,*
p 91, # 4

p 30 Of the two women I love   *Polo/Caña*. Associated with Silverio.
Machado y Alvarez. *Colección,*
p 184, # 6

p 31 For the man whose love   *Soleá*. Machado y Alvarez. *Colección,*
p 27, # 10

p 32 I asked God for vitality   *Soleá*. Pohren. *Lives,* p 111

p 33 Until my heart has broken   *Soleá*. Associated with Antonio el de
San Roque. Pohren. *Lives,* p 68

p 34 One dark night   *Serrana*. Associated with Silverio.
Machado y Alvarez. *Colección,*
p 202, # 7

p 35 When I loved you most   (*Soleá*). Fernández Bañuls. *La Poesía,*
p 92, # 5

p 36 By the light of the little cigar   (*Siguiriya*) Fernández Bañuls. *La Poesía,*
p 244, # 5

p 37 I shot at the sea   (*Soleá*). Fernández Bañuls. *La Poesía,*
p 244, # 6

p 38 If I don't come in life   (*Siguiriya*). Blanco Garza. *Las Letras,* p 26
p 39 According to Alvarez Caballero   Text. Alvarez Caballero, *Historia,* p 48
p 39 Past the Gates of Earth   *Siguiriya*. Alvarez Caballero, *Historia,* p 49
p 40 So, somewhere around three   Text. Pepe de la Matrona. Comellas.
Silverio, p 9

p 41 I went out to an olive grove   *Siguiriya*. Associated with Silverio.
Machado, *Colección,* p 190, # 4

p 42 Just like the Jews   (*Soleá*). Fernández Bañuls. *La Poesía,*
p 86, # 1

p 43   I asked death   (*Soleá*). Fernández Bañuls. *La Poesía*, p 72, # 6

p 44   When I'm up on the hill   (*Toná*). Fernández Bañuls. *La Poesía*, p 256, # 2

p 45   They took me out of one jail   (*Toná*). Fernández Bañuls. *La Poesía*, p 256, # 6

p 46   The voice of Silverio   Text. Alvarez Caballero. *Historia*, p 77

p 46   Any damn tongue   *Siguiriya*. Associated with Silverio. Alvarez Caballero. *Historia*, p 77

p 47   When I go to my room   *Siguiriya*. Associated with Silverio. Machado y Alvarez, *Colección*, p 184, # 3

p 48   Half Italian/half flamenco   Poem. García Lorca. *Poema de cante jondo*, p 95.

p 50   When I hear your name   *Siguiriya*. Associated with Silverio. Machado y Alvarez. *Colección*, p 184, # 4

p 51   The Gypsy *siguiriya* begins   Text. García Lorca quoted in Grande. *García Lorca*, p 53

p 52   My griefs are so enormous   *Siguiriya*. Molina. *Cante*, p 111

p 53   When the daylight comes   *Siguiriya*. Molina. *Cante*, p 112

p 54   Let the earth open   *Siguiriya*. Molina. *Cante*, p 112

p 55   My hand hurts   *Siguiriya*. Molina. *Cante*, p 111

p 56   If the dead could be raised   *Polo/Caña*. Associated with Silverio. Machado y Alvarez. *Colección*, p 186

p 57   You killed my brother   *Siguiriya*. Alvarez Caballero. *Historia*, p 53

p 58   Caballero Bonald tells   Text. Caballero Bonald quoted in Grande. *Memoria*, p 56

p 59   I'm not sorry that you're going   *Soleá*. Associated with Tía Anica la Piriñaca. Pohren. *Lives*, p 65

p 60   I leave the door ajar   (*Soleá*). Blanco Garza. *Las Letras*, p 23

p 61   Everyone prays to a goddess   *Siguiriya*. Associated with Silverio. Machado y Alvarez. *Colección*, p 198, # 65

p 62 Death came to my bedside Soleá. Pohren. *The Art*. p 146
p 63 I am living in this world Soleá. Pohren. *The Art*. p 146
p 64 One night of thunder *Siguiriya*. Associated with Silverio. Machado y Alvarez. *Colección*, p 199, # 3
p 65 It was said of Enrique Text. Alvarez Caballero. *Historia*, p 103
p 65 I leaned over the wall Siguiriya. Alvarez Caballero. *Historia*, p 103
p 66 There is nothing to see (*Soleá*). Blanco, Garza. *Las Letras*, p 29
p 67 It was in Tomelloso Text. Grande. *Memoria I*, p 19
p 68 To the mountains of Armenia *Siguiriya*. Associated with Silverio. Machado y Alvarez. *Colección*, p 189, # 1
p 69 All who deserve it Soleá. Pohren. *Lives*, p 47
p 70 I hope you get shot Soleá. Associated with Silverio. Machado y Alvarez. *Colección*, p 27, # 12
p 71 The figure of the *cantaor* Text. García Lorca, "Importancia histórica. . .del cante jondo" in García Lorca. *Poema*, p 162
p 71 Deceitful world Soleá. Associated with El Tenazas. Pohren. *Lives*, p 72
p 72 The sheep were white and small (*Siguiriya*). Blanco Garza. *Las Letras*, p 21
p 73 I don't ask anyone for favors (*Soleá*). Fernández Bañuls. *La Poesía*, p 257, # 5
p 74 Your mother keeps on saying (*Soleá*). Fernández Bañuls. *La Poesía*, p 258, # 5
p 75 Your mother keeps on saying (*Soleá*). Fernández Bañuls. *La Poesía*, p 258, # 6
p 76 Whenever I missed you (*Soleá*). Fernández Bañuls. *La Poesía*, p 90, # 1
p 77 Don't come to the forge (*Soleá*). Fernández Bañuls. *La Poesía*, p 246, # 2

101

p 78 That night in January   (*Soleá*). Fernández Bañuls. *La Poesía*,
                                       p 80, # 2
p 79 Come early my love   (*Soleá*). Fernández Bañuls. *La Poesía*,
                                       p 257, # 3
p 80 Then La Niña de los Peines   Text. García Lorca in *"Juego y teoria del
                                       duende"* in Alvarez Caballero.
                                       Historia, p 173
p 81 To your side   (*Siguiriya*). Fernández Bañuls. *La Poesía*,
                                       p 248, # 1
p 82 Love slopes steeply up   *Soleá*. Pohren. *The Art*, p 146
p 83 I went to a field to cry   (*Soleá*). Fernández Bañuls. *La Poesía*,
                                       p 248, # 4
p 84 Flamenco is tragedy   Text. José Monleon, in Grande. *García
                                       Lorca*, p 66
p 84 Though you go to hell   (*Soleá*). Fernández Bañuls. *La Poesía*,
                                       p 250, # 1
p 85 By the light of the candle   (*Soleá*). Fernández Bañuls. *La Poesía*,
                                       p 252, # 4
p 86 Lift your voice high, rosemary (*Soleá*). Fernández Bañuls. *La Poesía*,
                                       p 254, # 2
p 87 My heart was arrested   (*Soleá*). Fernández Bañuls. *La Poesía*,
                                       p 254, # 6
p 88 … and now, with the imminent Text. Antonio Mairena in Alvarez
                                       Caballero. *Historia*, p 12
p 89 Friends, now there are no   (*Soleá*). Fernández Bañuls. *La Poesía*,
      friends   p 255, # 2
p 90 I can do no more   (*Soleá*). Blanco Garza. *Las Letras*, p 22
p 91 Every morning I go by   (*Soleá*). Quoted by García Lorca in
                                       *"Importancia histórica … del cante
                                       jondo"* in García Lorca. *Poema*, p 155
p 92 At the banks of a river   (*Soleá*). Fernández Bañuls. *La Poesía*,
                                       p 246, # 1
p 93 Beneath a slender tree one day (*Soleá*). Fernández Bañuls. *La Poesía*,
                                       p 252, # 5

p 94 Beneath a barren tree   (*Soleá*). Fernández Bañuls. *La Poesía*,
                                     p 252, # 6
p 95 When asked why he sang   Text. Grande, *Agenda*, p18
p 95 At twelve o'clock or one   (*Soleá*). Fernández Bañuls. *La Poesía*,
                                     p 246, # 5
p 96 Though I tear off   (*Soleá*). Fernández Bañuls. *La Poesía*,
                                     p 72, # 3

BIBLIOGRAPHY

Alvarez Caballero, Angel. *Historia del Cante Flamenco*. Madrid: Alianza Editorial, 1981.

Blanco Garza, José Luis, et al. *Las Letras del Cante*. Sevilla: Signatura Ediciones de Andalucía, 1998.
A very nice little book, one of the few to discuss the place of *cante* as poetry, rather than as song or as part of the song–dance–guitar phenomenon.

Comellas, José Luis, et al. *Silverio Franconetti: 100 años de que murio y aun vive*. Sevilla: Ayuntamiento de Sevilla, 1989.

Fernández Bañuls, Juan Alberto. *La Poesía Flamenca Lírica en Andaluz*. Sevilla: Consejería de Cultura, Junta de Andalucia, 1983.
Difficult to obtain. Monumental collection of *cante* lyrics. Organized in curious fashion: in alphabetical order by opening words, three-line verses preceeding four-line verses. No notation of whether *siguiriya, soleá*, etc. A prologue in the form of an analysis by Franciso López Estrada. One section is titled "El feedback."

García Lorca, Federico. *Poema del cante jondo*. Edición de Mario Hernández. Madrid: Alianza Editorial, 1998.
A collection of sets of poems Lorca wrote in homage to flamenco. The sets are named after some of the types of *cante jondo*: the *siguiriya*, the *soleá*, the *saeta*. This edition also contains the essay he delivered in 1922 at a flamenco conference he organized with Manuel de Falla in Granada: "The Historical and Artistic

Importance of the Primitive Andaluz Song Called 'Cante Jondo.'"

Grande, Félix. *Agenda flamenca*. Sevilla: Editoriales Andaluzas Unidas, nd.

A collection of essays and talks given by the author over many years. Like his major work on flamenco, *Memoria del Flamenco*, this is both erudite and polemical, and a wonderful tour of flamenco by a devoted student of the *cante* and the guitar, as well as a first-rate writer.

Grande, Félix. *García Lorca y el Flamenco*. Madrid: Mondadori España, 1992.

Here, Grande both praises Lorca and criticizes some of his claims and understanding of flamenco. Rich with examples and citations of youthful Lorca letters, this work expands and deepens our understanding of the poet and of the *cante*.

Grande, Félix. *Memoria del Flamenco*. Madrid : Grande, Espasa-Calpe, 1979.

Two volumes. Memoirs by one of Spain's literary mavericks. Very very good.

Machado y Alvarez, Antonio. *Colección de Cantes Flamenco*. Sevilla: Imprenta El Porvenir, 1881. (Later editions by Ediciones Demófilo, Madrid, 1975.)

The first serious collection of *cante* by the father of the well-known poet Antonio Machado. Many good footnotes. Indispensable book.

Mercado, José. *La Seguidilla Gitana.* Madrid: Taurus Ediciones, 1982.

A study of *cante flamenco* that traces lineages of the various styles and analyzes metrics and rhyme schemes. A long section on the early *seguidillas.*

Molina, Ricardo. *Cante Flamenco.* Madrid: Taurus Ediciones, 1981.

Theory and history of *cante,* with an overview of some forty types. Includes a good selection of songs.

Pohren, Donn E. *The Art of Flamenco.* Jerez de la Frontera: Society of Spanish Studies, 1962.

An often praised early work, looking at the *flamenco puro* of southern Spain.

Pohren, D. E. *Lives and Legends of Flamenco: A Biographical History.* Sevilla: Society of Spanish Studies, 1964.

Story of flamenco's creators, developers, and interpreters. Useful bios of singers, musicians, and dancers. Photos.

DISCOGRAPHY

In the past few years more flamenco has become available in the U.S. I have generally been able to find CDs in Tower Records and in specialty music stores and guitar shops. Of course, when you are looking for recorded flamenco you will most often find guitar music — often without the voice. While that is fine, if that is what you are looking for, you will want to specify vocal for *cante jondo.*

One very good series is from France on the Le Chant du Monde label, distributed by Harmonia Mundi. It includes La Niña de Los Peines, Antonio Mairena, and a dozen other singers. The series concentrates on the classics — singers born near the turn of the last century — and has slim but helpful liner notes, at least in the latest releases. There are no translations of the lyrics. While Harmonia Mundi is at http://www.harmoniamundi.com. Le Chant du Monde does not have a site, but its e-mail address is cdm@harmoniamundi.com. I have not seen a complete catalog of the label.

Some of the albums are also issued in sets of 4, such as *Grandes Figures du Flamenco* (CMX 3741073.76), which includes the single CDs of: Beni de Cádiz; Rafael Romero; Tía Anica La Piriñaca (quoted in the book), and Juan Talega. The Tía Anica album is the only recording made of her voice. (Le Chant Du Monde LDX 2741028)

Another very good CD is *Cante Gitano: Gypsy Flamenco from Andalucia.* (Nimbus. NI 5168) It is a very clean digital recording made on site in Morón de la Frontera, near Seville, in August of 1988. The lyrics are printed in Spanish and in accurate, but uninspired, English.

Nimbus has other recordings of flamenco in its World Music series, which I haven't listened to. They can be found listed on the www.nimbus.ltd.uk/nrl site in the World Music section. In fact, you can even listen to some of the tracks with Real Audio. No mention is made in the descriptions of whether lyrics are printed.

El Cante Flamenco (Philips 832 531–2) This is a 3 CD set. The first is "Cante Basico" with such singers as Manolo Caracol and Antonio Mairena. The second is "The Golden Age." The third is more recent work. No notes of any kind.

Cante Flamenco: Agujetas en Paris (Radio France C 560012.) The two *bulerías* translated in this volume come from this album. The lyrics are printed in French and Spanish, not in English, although the titles are listed in English and there is a brief bio of Agujetas.

Arte Flamenco is the title of a collection under the Mandala imprint, and distributed by Harmonia Mundi of France. There are 12 volumes in the collection, plus a digital catalog which has excerpts from the 12 volumes. The catalog volume (MAN 4873) includes cuts of La Niña de los Peines and one of the earliest singers captured on wax cylinders, Juan Breva.

Arte Flamenco, vol. 12 (Man 4885) is another of the above series, and features El Niño de Cabra, El Soto, and others. No lyrics but short bios of the singers in French, Spanish and English.

L'Orient de l'Occident (Al Sur ALCD 131) is another CD from France and not flamenco, but a particularly wonderful homage to Ibn Arabi, Andalusian Sufi philsopher (1165–1240). The flamenco and Sufi musicians play works related to *cante jondo* and demonstrate Arabic roots.

Festival Flamenco Gitano 1 Live (CDLR 44.003) see *Cante chica*. Includes some *rhumba gitana, tientos, fandangos, bulerías*. Very lively, with *jalea* and hand clapping.

Pedro Bacan: Alurican (Le Chant du Monde LDX 274906) More strictly guitar—little or no voice. Includes *soleares, siguiriya, bulerías,* and others.

WORLD WIDE WEBOGRAPHY

There is a lot of information on the World Wide Web. A search on "Flamenco" will turn up hundreds of pages, including German and Japanese flamenco pages. These are only a few of the sites available:

www.elpais.com. This is a major Spanish newspaper, and one of the listings on its web site is "Flamenco." There are a good dozen links to other sites, all in Spanish.

www.flamenco-world.com both sells and has information on events, artists, styles. Either Spanish or English text can be found. A magazine is one of its offerings.

www.flamenco.org is a small site, run by a single person. It has some leads and connections and encourages contributions from its readers, but is somewhat thin. No lists of books or recordings.

http://www.lingolex.com/flamenco.htm is The Flamenco Record shop associated with Amazon.com. You can order directly, but as with much on Amazon.com there is no detail about the artists or songs on a specific recording.